J972.

JUNE 2021

The library is always open at
renfrewshirelibraries.co.uk

Visit now for
homework help
and free
eBooks.

We are the Skoobs and we love the library!

Phone: **0300 300 1188**
Email: **libraries@renfrewshire.gov.uk**

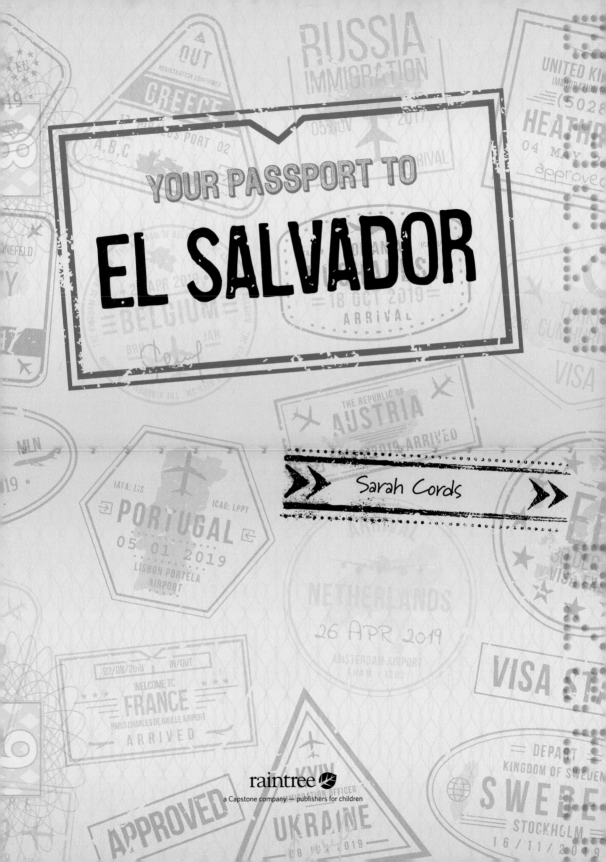

YOUR PASSPORT TO

EL SALVADOR

Sarah Cords

raintree
a Capstone company — publishers for children

Raintree is an imprint of Capstone Global Library Limited, a company incorporated in England and Wales having its registered office at 264 Banbury Road, Oxford, OX2 7DY – Registered company number: 6695582

www.raintree.co.uk
myorders@raintree.co.uk

Edited by Jamie Hudalla
Designed by Colleen McLaren
Original illustrations © Capstone Global Library Limited 2021
Originated by Capstone Global Library Ltd
Printed and bound in India

978 1 3982 0547 5 (hardback)
978 1 3982 0548 2 (paperback)

British Library Cataloguing in Publication Data
A full catalogue record for this book is available from the British Library.

Acknowledgements
We would like to thank the following for permission to reproduce photographs: AP Images: Richard Drew, 13; iStockphoto: lanabyko, cover (bottom); Newscom: Album/Oronoz, 10; Red Line Editorial: 5; Shutterstock Images: carlos.araujo, 27, Daniel Andis, 9, Danita Delmont, 12, De Jongh Photography, 11, Filip Bjorkman, cover (map), Guayo Fuentes, 17, 28, HMedia, 7, Joey Villaflor, 6, Kobby Dagan, 18, Millenius, 25, Milosz Maslanka, 15, 21, StudioGShock, 22, Thiago B Trevisan, 19, Wee design, cover (flag)
Design Elements: iStockphoto, Shutterstock Images

We would like to thank Professor Cecilia Menjívar, Dorothy L. Meier Social Equities Chair at the University of California, USA, for her assistance in the preparation of this book.

Every effort has been made to contact copyright holders of material reproduced in this book. Any omissions will be rectified in subsequent printings if notice is given to the publisher.

CONTENTS

Words in **bold** are in the glossary.

CHAPTER ONE

WELCOME TO EL SALVADOR!

A tall volcano towers over San Salvador. Beautiful churches and buildings line the streets. The city has many art museums. San Salvador is high in the mountains. It is the capital of El Salvador.

El Salvador is located in Central America. The country is nestled between Honduras and Guatemala. It could fit inside the UK about 12 times. More than 6 million people live there. Its climate is **tropical**. The temperature is mostly hot. The rainy season is from May to October. During this time, rain falls nearly every day.

MAP OF EL SALVADOR

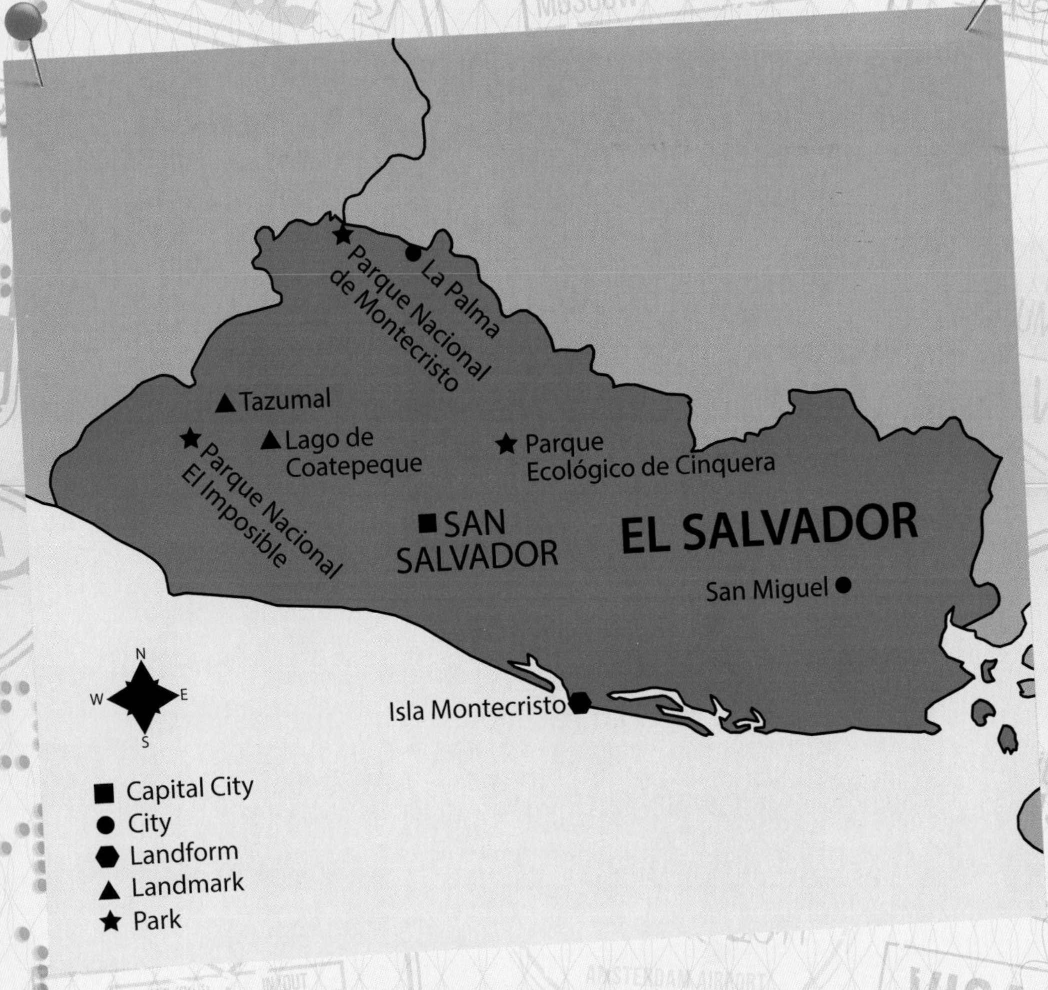

Parque Nacional
de Montecristo

La Palma

▲ Tazumal

▲ Lago de
Coatepeque

★ Parque
Ecológico de Cinquera

★ Parque Nacional
El Imposible

■ SAN
SALVADOR

EL SALVADOR

San Miguel ●

Isla Montecristo

N
W ◆ E
S

- ■ Capital City
- ● City
- ⬡ Landform
- ▲ Landmark
- ★ Park

Explore El Salvador's
cities and landmarks.

5

San Salvador has beautiful, old buildings.

Most of the people who live in El Salvador are *mestizo*. They have both European and **indigenous ancestors**. Some people speak native languages such as Nawat and Nahuatl. Others speak Spanish. Spanish is the country's official language.

Visitors can find beautiful natural areas in El Salvador. The country has parks with rare flowers and birds. People love to hike in the mountains. They can also surf in the Pacific Ocean.

FACT

More than 400 species of birds live in El Salvador.

People can surf off El Salvador's coast.

FACT FILE

OFFICIAL NAME: REPUBLIC OF EL SALVADOR

POPULATION: 6,187,271

LAND AREA: 21,040 SQ. KM (8,124 SQ. MI)

CAPITAL: SAN SALVADOR

MONEY: US DOLLAR AND SALVADORAN COLÓN

GOVERNMENT: Republic, with a president as the head of the government.

LANGUAGE: SPANISH, NAWAT AND NAHUATL

GEOGRAPHY: El Salvador is located between Honduras and Guatemala. It is mountainous, with two ranges that run side by side in the middle of the country.

NATURAL RESOURCES: El Salvador has wood, cattle, sugar cane, coffee, cotton and corn.

CHAPTER TWO

HISTORY OF EL SALVADOR

For 10,000 years, people have lived in the region that is now El Salvador. A group of people called the Olmecs settled there as early as 2000 **BCE**. Then, people from Mexico arrived in the 1000s **CE**. They were known as the Pipils. They called the land Cuscatlán. From 1000 BCE to the 1500s CE, people of the **Maya** civilization also lived there. They built roads and cities in the area.

SPANISH RULE

In 1524, Pedro de Alvarado arrived from Spain. He started a war with the Pipils. Spain wanted the land for its gold, agricultural products and farm land. This would make Spain wealthier. By 1528, the Spanish invaders had won the war. The Spanish named the region El Salvador.

People can visit the remains of Maya farmhouses in El Salvador.

Pedro de Alvarado took control of El Salvador in the early 1500s.

In 1808, the emperor of France invaded Spain. The war in Spain weakened the control of the Spanish throughout Central America. In 1821, the people of El Salvador declared their **independence**.

A statue of General Gerardo Barrios stands in San Salvador.

In 1824, El Salvador joined the Federal Republic of Central America. Guatemala, Nicaragua, Costa Rica and Honduras belonged to this group. The leaders of this republic could not agree on how to rule. In 1841, El Salvador left this group. It became a **sovereign** nation.

COFFEE BEANS AND CIVIL WARS

In 1858, General Gerardo Barrios became El Salvador's president. He decided growing and selling coffee to other countries would make more money for the country.

Coffee beans grow on coffee plants.

FACT

In 2019, more than 150,000 farmers grew coffee in El Salvador.

By the 1920s, coffee was the country's main crop. Coffee made up 90 per cent of El Salvador's **exports** to other countries.

Nayib Bukele became
El Salvador's president in 2019.

In the 1980s, a civil war broke out. At that time, the military and government had too much control. People with little money or power fought for more rights. The war lasted 12 years. Many people fled the country. When the war ended, people tried to live together peacefully. In 2019, Nayib Bukele became president. Presidents can stay in office for five years in El Salvador.

CHAPTER THREE

EXPLORE EL SALVADOR

El Salvador has ancient landmarks, vibrant towns and natural areas. The Maya built an ancient settlement called Tazumal. It has several pyramids. Other remains of the city have been discovered. These include ball courts and statues.

La Palma is a town in the Sierra Madre mountain range. The town is known for its art and **murals**. There are many hiking trails with pine trees around it. Other towns lie along the coast. Costa del Sol and El Tunco are coastal towns. They have popular beaches.

Tourists can visit the impressive Maya structures at Tazumal.

PARKS AND RESERVES

PARQUE NACIONAL DE MONTECRISTO: Located in the mountainous region of the country. Some animals that don't live anywhere else in the country live in this park.

ISLA MONTECRISTO: A tiny island in the Pacific, just off the coast. It is a wonderful place to watch birds.

PARQUE NACIONAL EL IMPOSIBLE: A forest park that contains more than 400 types of trees and 100 types of mammals.

PARQUE ECOLÓGICO DE CINQUERA: A park with nearly 4,000 hectares (10,000 acres), roughly the size of 7,500 football fields! It is located near Cinquera, a historical village.

MOUNTAINS AND VOLCANOES

Mountains cover El Salvador. The country is sometimes called the Land of Volcanoes. It has more than 20 active volcanoes. One of the most beautiful lakes in El Salvador is Lago de Coatepeque. Coatepeque is a volcano. Thousands of years ago, the volcano erupted. A crater formed in its side. Over time, the crater filled with water. It became a lake.

When Coatepeque erupted, it formed a crater that filled with water.

VOLCANOES

The volcanoes in El Salvador are part of the Pacific Ring of Fire. One of the most famous parks in the country features several volcanoes. This is the Cerro Verde National Park. While there, visitors can walk up two volcanoes, Izalco and Santa Ana. Santa Ana is the tallest volcano in the country.

The government once had offices in the National Palace in San Salvador.

THE CAPITAL CITY

The capital of El Salvador is San Salvador. More than 2 million people live in and near the city. Although the city was built in 1528, not all of its buildings are old. Because of earthquakes, many parts of the city have been rebuilt. Today, San Salvador has beautiful buildings, such as a large cathedral called Catedral Metropolitana.

Catedral Metropolitana was opened to the public in 1999.

CHAPTER FOUR

DAILY LIFE

Many people in El Salvador live outside the cities. Farms scatter the plains of the country. A lot of farmers grow coffee. Some of these farmers work together. They form coffee cooperatives. These cooperatives help them earn more money for their coffee.

MINING

Gold and copper mining used to be part of El Salvador's **economy**. But in 2017, a law was passed that banned mining. Many people worked together to pass this law. Citizens and government leaders thought the ban was a good idea. Mining can cause damage to the environment. The people of El Salvador hoped this ban would protect their environment.

Farmers spread out coffee beans to dry in the Sun.

Many people put pork and cheese in pupusas.

TRADITIONAL CLOTHES AND FOOD

People often wear light clothing. The lightweight fabric helps the wearer stay cool in the country's hot weather. Traditional clothing often has embroidery, or decorations made with needles and thread. These outfits are usually colourful and are worn when performing traditional dances.

FACT

One of El Salvador's exports is indigo. This blue dye comes from the anil plant.

A popular food is *pupusa*. Corn tortillas make up the outside of pupusas. People fill the tortillas with beans, pork and cheese.

THE SCHOOL SYSTEM

Children in El Salvador usually start school at the age of seven. Some children can attend up to nine years of school. Then they can leave or go on to get their final years of secondary school education. They may then go to university. Many go to the Universidad de El Salvador. It was founded in 1841. It is one of the best universities in the country.

FRESCO DE ENSALADA DE FRUTAS

Fresco de ensalada de frutas is a traditional fruit salad drink. Ask an adult for help preparing the fruit for this recipe.

Ingredients:

- 432 g tin of crushed pineapple
- 2 apples, cut into small pieces
- 2 oranges, peeled and cut into small pieces
- 60 ml orange juice
- A splash of lemon juice
- 125 g of cantaloupe melon cut into small pieces
- 50 g sugar
- 2 litres water
- A pinch of salt

Method:

1. Combine pineapples, apples, oranges and cantaloupe melon in large bowl.
2. Add orange juice, lemon juice, sugar, water and pinch of salt.
3. Stir and then refrigerate for one hour.

CHAPTER FIVE

HOLIDAYS AND CELEBRATIONS

15 September is Día de la Independencia. The people of El Salvador celebrate their independence from Spain. People march in parades. At night, they let off colourful fireworks.

A popular indigenous celebration is the Día de la Cruz. This holiday is celebrated at the beginning of the rainy season, on 3 May. People decorate crosses with flowers and make offerings of fruit. They honour the land and celebrate the harvest.

RELIGIOUS HOLIDAYS

In El Salvador, 80 per cent of people are Christians. About half of the people who live there are Roman Catholics. Even if people do not belong to a religion, some still celebrate religious holidays.

On Día de la Independencia, people wave El Salvador's flag during military marches.

Many Catholics honour saints. In the Catholic religion, saints are people who are considered very holy. In the city of San Miguel, people celebrate the Queen of the Peace Day. It takes place on the last Saturday in November. It is a day to honour Mary, the mother of Jesus. Mary is very important to Catholics.

CHAPTER SIX

SPORT AND RECREATION

Football is the most popular sport in El Salvador. There are 10 teams in the country's top league. One football stadium in San Salvador can hold 45,000 fans. That is half the amount of fans that Wembley Stadium can hold.

Adventure sports are also popular in El Salvador. People enjoy walking in the mountains. For those who live near the sea, people often swim and surf in the Pacific Ocean's big waves. Many people also go kayaking on the beautiful lakes.

TYPES OF MUSIC

Salvadorans listen to a variety of music. Many people know songs that have been passed down by their ancestors.

There are many mountains and volcanoes to hike in El Salvador.

Musicians perform at Puerta de la Libertad in El Salvador.

One type of music is called cumbia of El Salvador. This music mixes African, Spanish and indigenous styles. Some people also enjoy Salvadoran hip-hop.

From its vibrant towns to its tall volcanoes, there is a lot to see in El Salvador. With its delicious food and beautiful views, El Salvador is a wonderful place to visit and live.

TRIPA CHUCA

Tripa Chuca is a game played by children in El Salvador. To play, you need two people, paper and two different coloured marker or felt-tip pens.

1. All over the paper, in random order, write the numbers 1 to 20 in one pen colour.
2. On the same sheet of paper, repeat step one with the other colour.
3. The first player circles number one and then draws a line to the number one in the other colour and circles it.
4. The second player uses the other colour pen and circles number two. The second player draws a line to the other number two and circles it. But the line that that player draws cannot touch or cross the line the first player drew.
5. The players take turns in circling and connecting the numbers in sequence. Eventually things get very messy!
6. The player who touches another number or line first loses.

GLOSSARY

ancestor
family member who lived a
long time ago

BCE/CE
BCE means Before
Common Era, or before
year one. CE means
Common Era, or after
year one.

economy
wealth and resources in
a country

export
sell and ship products to
other countries

independence
freedom a country has to
govern itself

indigenous
first people, plants and
animals to live in a country

Maya
nation of people in Mexico
and Central America that
lived from 7000 BCE to
1524 CE

mural
large painting usually
created on a wall or
large surface

sovereign
independent and
governing itself

tropical
climate that is very hot
and humid

FIND OUT MORE

BOOKS

Daily Life in the Maya Civilization (Daily Life in Ancient Civilizations), Nick Hunter (Raintree, 2016)

Maya, Incas, and Aztecs, Brian Williams (DK Children, 2018)

South America: Everything You Ever Wanted to Know (Not For Parents), Lonely Planet Kids (Lonely Planet Kids, 2014)

WEBSITES

kids.nationalgeographic.com/explore/countries/el-salvador
Explore more about El Salvador with National Geographic.

www.dkfindout.com/uk/earth/volcanoes/where-are-earths-volcanoes
Find out more about the Earth's volanoes on this website.

INDEX

OTHER BOOKS IN THIS SERIES

YOUR PASSPORT TO CHINA
YOUR PASSPORT TO ECUADOR
YOUR PASSPORT TO ETHIOPIA
YOUR PASSPORT TO FRANCE
YOUR PASSPORT TO IRAN
YOUR PASSPORT TO KENYA
YOUR PASSPORT TO PERU
YOUR PASSPORT TO RUSSIA
YOUR PASSPORT TO SPAIN